The Tarka Trail Guide

Carl & Gigha Klinkenborg

Printed in the UK

ISBN: 978-0-9932376-0-7

Published by Westside Warehouse Books

Bideford, Devon EX39 2AZ

tarkatrailguide.co.uk

Contents   Page

Introduction

The Tarka Trail in its entirety is a 290km figure '8' shaped long-distance route centered roughly on the town of Barnstaple in North Devon. It encompasses roads, footpaths, bridleways and cycleways. This guide focusses on the shared-use section; a completely car-free route for use by walkers, cyclists and horse riders. Following the route of a former railway line, the Tarka Trail was officially opened on 28th May 1992 by H.R.H. The Prince of Wales, and has become one of the 'must visit' places in North Devon. The Trail traces the journeys of 'Tarka the Otter', taking in locations featured in the 1927 classic novel by Henry Williamson.

We have written this guide travelling from north to south, ie. Braunton to Meeth. Should you be exploring in the opposite direction, you will need to reverse any instructions and points of interest.

In the old railway days, there would have been few trees close to the line. Now the Tarka Trail is a veritable wildlife corridor – a haven for butterflies and bats, dormice, otters and countless wild flowers and plant species.

Enjoy a car-free journey on foot, by bicycle, wheelchair, buggy or on horseback. The Trail is largely flat and the surface, mostly tarmac, is suitable for all the family. We live in Bideford, which is roughly in the middle of this shared-use section of the Trail; we count ourselves very lucky to be able to enjoy regular walking and cycling adventures, and all this beautiful countryside has to offer.

So get on your bike - hire one if you don't have your own - or take a leisurely walk through 48km of stunning North Devon countryside and see it through enlightened eyes. We think it is the best recreational route in North Devon. There is so much to see along the route, and this guide will ensure you don't miss any 'proper gems'.

Audio Discovery Posts

There are 21 discovery posts spread along the length of the shared-use section. Each post links to an audio clip that can be downloaded onto your phone, tablet or audio player. Play these clips at the corresponding discovery post to learn about the wildlife, history and railway heritage of the Tarka Trail.

1. Velator wetland
2. Mud
3. On the verge
4. From rail to Trail
5. Salt marsh
6. Farming for wildlife
7. Fremington cuttings
8. Fremington trade
9. RSPB Isley Marsh
10. Instow pond
11. Lime kilns
12. Tides
13. Rolle Canal
14. Otters
15. Salmon
16. Bats
17. Coppice
18. Dormice
19. Culm grassland
20. Butterflies
21. Woodlands

Scan this QR code with your mobile phone to download the audio clips

Code of Conduct

The shared-use section of the Tarka Trail is enjoyed by many different people - walkers, cyclists, wheelchair/mobility scooter users, dog walkers and horse riders. Please follow these simple guidelines:

Keep left When using the Trail, if you keep left, everyone can travel more safely. It makes passing other users easier and reduces 'traffic jams' at busy times.

Give Way Cyclists should always give way to all other users.

Ring a bell Your bike should have a bell fitted. Make sure other Tarka Trail users are aware of your presence. Ring your bell or call out a warning.

Relax Please keep your speed down; the Trail is not a racing track. Slow down, relax and enjoy the scenery.

Look During peak times the Trail is used by many more cyclists than walkers. If walking, take care; if you are using headphones, improve your visual awareness.

Dogs Please keep dogs under control at all times. The Trail is a haven for wildlife, which is vulnerable to disturbance. Do not allow your dog to interfere with cyclists by getting in their way or chasing them. Do not allow your dog onto adjacent farmland. Dog mess is unpleasant for everyone. Please clean up after your dog and use the bins along the Trail. Please don't throw filled bags in the hedges.

Horses The Tarka Trail is used by horses between Torrington Servis Farm and Meeth Halt, so please approach and pass considerately.

Please be considerate to other users; think about their enjoyment as well as your own.

Follow the Country Code, please don't litter, and remember to close all gates behind you.

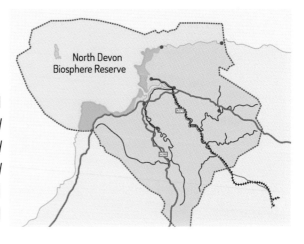

North Devon Biosphere Reserve

North Devon is so special that UNESCO, *the United Nations Educational and Scientific and Cultural Organisation,* designated the region as a World Biosphere Reserve.

Why? North Devon has three very special qualities:

- Special landscapes and wildlife areas
- A rich cultural heritage
- Communities who care about living sustainably

Biosphere Reserves have three main functions:

- Learning and research
- Sustainable development
- Conservation

A partnership of 28 organisations have come together to carry out these functions, which includes the management of the Tarka Trail.

It was the first area in the UK to be designated as such and covers a staggering 3300km^2 of land and sea, and is home to 150 000 people. The core area is the sand dune system of Braunton Burrows. The Tarka Trail is entirely contained within the Biosphere Reserve, making it the perfect gateway from which to explore the area.

To find out more about the North Devon Biosphere, visit the Biosphere website: www.northdevonbiosphere.org.uk

**NORTH DEVON
COAST**
Areas of Outstanding
Natural Beauty

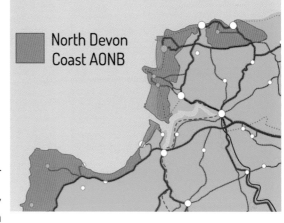

North Devon
Coast AONB

From the edge of Exmoor to the border of Cornwall, The North Devon Coast is a designated Area of Outstanding Natural Beauty (AONB). This designation recognises the very special landscape, habitats, wildlife and heritage of this area. It also enables our coastline to be enjoyed and developed sustainably, and in keeping with its natural beauty. This ensures that North Devon will remain as beautiful and special tomorrow, for future generations to enjoy, as it is for us today.

North Devon Coast AONB is rich in its distinctive characteristics, from rugged cliffs carved by the sea and capped by Iron Age hill forts, sheltered harbours and fishing villages to ancient burial mounds. The hamlets, farms and fields are steeped in history, and its oak woodlands are home to rare wildlife.

From the Tarka Trail in Braunton, you can explore the AONB. You can walk or cycle around to the sandy beach at Crow Point, or the internationally renowned sand dunes at Braunton Burrows. Take the summer ferry from Instow to Appledore and explore the coast down to Cornwall, or follow the National Cycle Network from Braunton up to the iconic Victorian fishing town of Ilfracombe, to discover the rocky cliffs and hidden beaches of the northern coast.

To find out more about the North Devon Coast AONB
visit the AONB website: www.explorethecoast.org

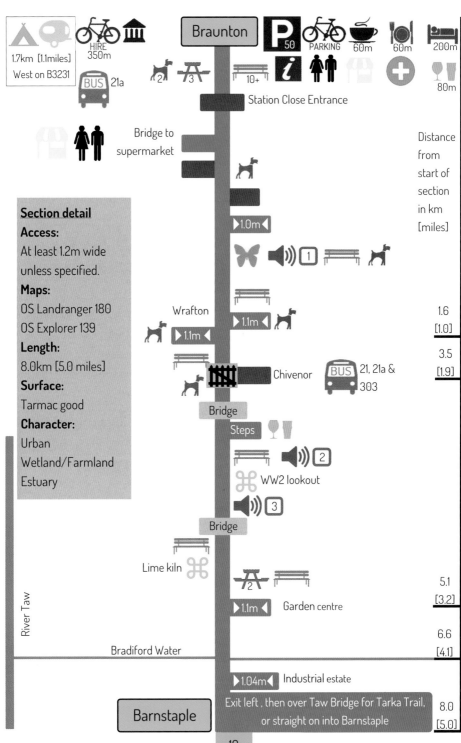

Braunton

1.7km [1.1miles]
West on B3231

HIRE 350m

BUS 21a

PARKING 50

60m 60m 200m

10+

80m

Station Close Entrance

Bridge to supermarket

Section detail
Access:
At least 1.2m wide unless specified.
Maps:
OS Landranger 180
OS Explorer 139
Length:
8.0km [5.0 miles]
Surface:
Tarmac good
Character:
Urban
Wetland/Farmland
Estuary

1.0m

Wrafton

1.1m

1.1m

1.6 [1.0]

3.5 [1.9]

Chivenor

BUS 21, 21a & 303

Bridge

Steps

2

WW2 lookout

3

Bridge

Lime kiln

River Taw

5.1 [3.2]

1.1m Garden centre

6.6 [4.1]

Bradiford Water

1.04m Industrial estate

Barnstaple

Exit left , then over Taw Bridge for Tarka Trail, or straight on into Barnstaple

8.0 [5.0]

Distance from start of section in km [miles]

10

Braunton to Barnstaple

Our journey along the wonderful Tarka Trail begins in a humble public car park near the centre of Braunton village. With the main road and flower-filled roundabout behind you, head towards the right-hand side of the car park until a path bordered by tall trees and a small river is reached. This unassuming path marks the start of our 48km adventure along this shared-use section of the Tarka Trail.

Bridge at Chivenor

It is difficult to imagine that around us once stood busy Braunton Station with its level crossing, stationmaster's house, two platforms and sidings. The most recognisable building remaining is the goods shed, now the Museum of British Surfing. The course of the railway around Braunton has been partially erased, having either been built upon or had new roads laid over it in several places, making this the trickiest part of the Trail to follow.

At most times, the River Caen beside the Trail in Braunton is a shallow and swiftly-flowing brook; however, it has overtopped its banks on many occasions, notably in December 2012. The previous June, improved flood defences nearby had been completed at a cost of £1m, but it was barely six months later that they were overwhelmed, resulting in much of the village centre being flooded knee-deep.

After following the path beside the river, we bear left away from it, taking direction from a signpost indicating *The Burrows* and *Barnstaple* and also marked as cycleway 27. Here we cross one of the few surviving remnants of track and turn right along Station Road.

We reach an old white-painted railway signal, looking somewhat out of place in the front garden of a modern house. Turn right into Station Close, then almost immediately left onto the Tarka Trail proper; now clearly an old railway line. Largely bordered by trees on both sides, the view to the right briefly opens out, revealing a new elevated footway built over a small floodplain of the river and leading to a superstore.

Velator Wetland

Chivenor

We soon come to a gate, and although our course lies dead ahead, we need to cross the road to our immediate right and follow the marked pavement around the roundabout 'the wrong way' to rejoin the Trail, after carefully crossing a minor road that can prove busy. Another gate marks the way back onto the Trail, after which point it becomes child's play to navigate.

We soon come to Velator Wetlands with its boardwalks extending right out into the water. There is a large pool, created during flood defence work, which then remained closed off for 8 years, naturally developing a diversity of plant and animal life before being managed and opened to the public in 2004. Viewing platforms and access points now allow this formerly hidden gem to be enjoyed by all. The resident birds are quite tame and provide excellent photographic opportunities, the migratory visitors being more shy.

Braunton & District Museum
The Bakehouse Centre,
Caen Street,
Braunton EX33 1AA
01271 816688

Bridge: Chivenor section

The water is often exceptionally clear, allowing the bottom to be easily seen, and the swans, duck sand geese seem to expect food from all visitors. Please resist the temptation to throw bread for them, as this can harm the water quality and is not a healthy option for wildfowl. On the opposite side of the Trail are flat fields and marshland that often flood, providing another, if transient, habitat for wildfowl. Reaching a gate, we are facing the old Wrafton Station building, now a house, which saw its last train pass through in 1970, and where we can see another railway signal standing in what is now a garden.

We dogleg right-left to rejoin the Trail through another gate, and notice on our right the first views of RMB Chivenor through its long perimeter fence. Built in the 1930s, it was later taken over by RAF Coastal Command, working with nearby RAF Northam's new-fangled 'Chain Home' long-range radar to detect and intercept high-flying enemy planes. It is home to the bright yellow Sea King Search and Rescue helicopters, which can often be seen from the Trail, parked on the apron behind the first hangar we see. Passing along 1.5km of security fence, we reach the Base entrance road that we cross carefully beside a roundabout.

Did you know?
The far bank of the River Taw is over 700m distant, and in places this estuary is five times wider than the Thames at Tower Bridge.

The Trail passes under a bridge and opens out, revealing the river Taw. With a tidal range of over 6m, the difference in views as the waters ebb and flow is dramatic, from a still, unbroken expanse of water to vast sandbanks, mudflats and swirling river channels.

Looking directly across the water with the moored boats to your right, you can see distant Fremington Quay, also on the Trail. We have to travel further inland to Barnstaple before the river is narrow enough for the bridge that was built in the late thirteenth century.

Taw Bridge, Barnstaple

The Trail closely follows the busy A361 for a while before veering away from it; however, the traffic noise rarely intrudes above the sounds of water and wildlife. Along this section are benches, a picnic area and grassy verges, ideal for a rest or picnic enjoying the wide views across the estuary. A few metres off the Trail, at the edge of a small grassy clearing, is a WW2 lookout hut; containing a bench, it is useful for wildfowl photography, particularly of the more shy species. The open banks of the river give way to a flood-wall protecting the low-lying land away from the river, with the industrial buildings to our left indicating that we are now nearing Barnstaple. The new 'downstream' bridge looms large, and since its opening in 2007, we must turn left shortly before it and follow the signpost *Bideford NCN27*. This takes us up and over the bridge on a dedicated cycle path, where some spectacular views are to be had from atop its 400m span.

Did you know?
The swing bridge across the route into Barnstaple, which opens to allow river traffic to enter the River Yeo on the left, has been designed to resemble a boat.

Long Bridge, Barnstaple

Barnstaple has much to offer, and can soon be reached by continuing straight on and under the bridge.

Barnstaple: an historic market town

For Barnstaple follow the cycleway straight on under the Taw Bridge, over the swing bridge and past the Civic Centre car park on the left. Keeping to the cycleway, zig-zag left and then right around the Old Barnstaple Railway Station, now a school, and back to the river's edge along The Strand. To your left, you will find Barnstaple Heritage Centre, plus bars, cafes and restaurants with outdoor seating. Continue on the cycleway under the bridge to reach The Square and the Museum of Barnstaple & North Devon.

To re-join the Tarka Trail, continue under the Long Bridge, then circle left around the museum and onto the bridge. Please take extra care, as on the bridge there is no cycleway, which starts again by Halfords. At the roundabout you can bear left, which leads to Barnstaple Station and Tarka Trail Cycle Hire, or straight ahead along Sticklepath Terrace. At the end, turn right and immediately right again, and continue under the road. Then turn left and go under the road again. You are now back on the Tarka Trail. Turn left for the next section: Barnstaple to Fremington.

Vintage cycle ride on the Tarka Trail

 5b, 8, 8a, 8e, 21, 21a, 71, 72, 75b, 85, 310 & 319

 100m

Barnstaple

  50 PARKING HIRE

Barnstaple Station

100m

Access to Petroc College
not restricted but steep

1.4
[0.9]

Anchorwood Bank
Development site

 Anchor Wood
Not suitable for wheelchairs

Section detail

Access:
At least 1.2m wide
unless specified.

OS maps:
Landranger 180
Explorer 139

Length :
4.8km [3 miles]

Surface:
Tarmac good/fair - some
uneven patches

Character:
Estuary
Salt marsh
Farmland

  4

2.7
[1.7]

⌘

 5

Distance
from
start of
section
in km
[miles]

⌘

  6

Footpath—no cycling

 2

4.0
[2.5]

 7

Fremington cuttings

Bridge

River Taw

 5b, 21, 21a, 903, 904 & x85

950m

 40 PARKING

 10+ 10

Fremington

 HIRE ℹ hire

4.8
[3.0]

16

Barnstaple to Fremington

After passing over the bridge, we roll down towards the roundabout with its controversial Devonian slate and steel art installation, officially named 'Barum Stenning' but known locally as Barnhenge or Sticklehenge, after Sticklepath Hill at whose foot it lies.

Tandem with trailer

We turn right before reaching the roundabout, away from the road and through a chicane of metal railings following the signpost *Town Centre/Bideford*. The path curves back towards the main road and a tunnel; however, we must bear sharp right just before this to continue along the Trail, signposted *Bideford* (this tunnel is the quickest and safest route by which to reach Barnstaple mainline railway station from the Trail). There is a useful interpretation board here, showing the Tarka Trail's route in its entirety, together with the routes of local circular walks. Also standing here is one of several cast iron waymarkers placed along the Trail where it is shared by the National Cycle Network. Known as 'Millennium Mileposts', they were commissioned by Sustrans.

As we travel along the tree-lined Trail, it soon opens out with views to the river, salt marshes and mudflats on one side and woodland and farmland on the other. Here there is a gated path to the right, heading back towards the bridge and Anchorwood Bank, but as of Spring 2015 it is a dead end due to redevelopment of the area beyond.

Directly opposite the gate is a nature trail through Anchor Wood County Wildlife Site, a small broadleaved woodland populated by ash, oak, cherry and Devon whitebeam. Walking the nature trail in the spring, we will see primrose and bluebells.

Little Egret

The mudflats uncovered at low tide contain an abundance of life, and are a vital feeding ground for curlew, oystercatchers and the inevitable gulls which flock here. Look out for the delightful Little Egret, a small white heron, which is common in North Devon and always a stunning sight. Many migratory species overwinter here, and the numbers of potential prey attract birds higher up the food chain, such as the peregrine falcon and sparrowhawk.

Along the length of the Trail, sculptures and artworks are dotted here and there, and we soon come across a most obvious example right in the centre of the Trail. If you study it carefully you will notice that it is built largely from old railway-related components. Take a moment to look at the salt marshes bordering the Trail along this section. These areas harbour particular plant species able to tolerate the salty conditions, and were traditionally rich grazing grounds for cattle and sheep, whose meat was said to be especially tasty. Also, the tidal creeks and pools allow fish to spawn in relatively sheltered waters. On the highest tides in spring and autumn the width of the river here is huge, reaching right up to the foot of the causeway on which the Trail runs, and depositing driftwood on its retreat.

Did you know?

Across the river to the north, we can see some of the giant wind turbines of Fullabrook wind farm, one of England's largest.
The 22 turbines began generating electricity in 2011, and at full capacity can power 30,000 homes .

Fremington cuttings

The long views finally give way to an enclosing railway cutting, and here we see the results that careful management of the verges has achieved. South-facing slopes have been favoured, to take maximum advantage of sunlight and warmth.

From springtime through the summer, this habitat is home to many varieties of wild flowers, such as primroses, oxeye daisies and early purple orchids and also attracts large numbers of brimstone and common blue butterflies. We pass under an impressive stone bridge, which carries only a farm track accessing a finger of land poking out into the estuary. Shortly thereafter we reach the still-busy Fremington Quay, where cyclists and walkers have replaced the ships and railway of quite different times.

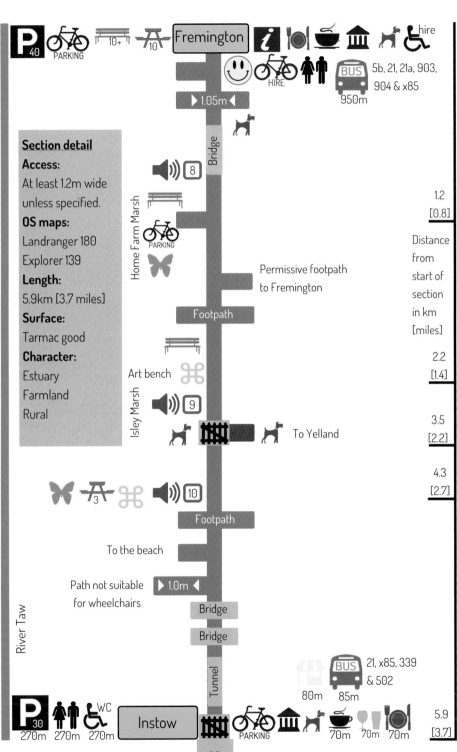

P 40 PARKING

🚲 10+ 🪑 🧺 10

Fremington

ℹ️ 🍽️ 🍜 🏛️ 🐕 ♿ hire

🙂 🚲 HIRE 🚻 🚌 **BUS** 5b, 21, 21a, 903, 904 & x85
950m

▶ 1.05m ◀

🐕

Bridge

🔊 8

Section detail
Access:
At least 1.2m wide
unless specified.
OS maps:
Landranger 180
Explorer 139
Length:
5.9km [3.7 miles]
Surface:
Tarmac good
Character:
Estuary
Farmland
Rural

Home Farm Marsh

🪑

🚲 PARKING

🦋

Permissive footpath
to Fremington

Footpath

🪑

1.2
[0.8]

Distance
from
start of
section
in km
[miles]

2.2
[1.4]

Art bench ⌘

Isley Marsh

🔊 9

🐕 ▦ 🐕 To Yelland

3.5
[2.2]

🦋 🧺 3 ⌘ 🔊 10

4.3
[2.7]

Footpath

To the beach

Path not suitable
for wheelchairs

▶ 1.0m ◀

River Taw

Bridge

Bridge

Tunnel

🏪 🚌 **BUS** 21, x85, 339 & 502

80m 85m

P 30 🚻 ♿ WC

270m 270m 270m

Instow ▦ 🚲 PARKING 🏛️ 🐕 ☕ 🍷 🍽️

70m 70m 70m

5.9
[3.7]

20

Fremington to Instow

Fremington Quay played a huge part in supporting the industry and growth of nearby Barnstaple, where the river Taw was silting up and thus unable to handle the larger ships of the mid-19th century. The deep-water quay built here was vital for offloading coal, lime and other heavy materials necessary for the town's growth. Although these were initially transported on the railway by horse-drawn wagons, steam trains arrived in 1855, opening up this part of North Devon to visitors from the whole country. Trains and ships remained active well into the 20th century, but the station closed in the late '60s, with the quay handling large amounts of local Peters Marland clay until somewhat later. There is an excellent Heritage Centre here, with a superb model railway display showing the area as it was in its heyday.

Fremington Quay

FREMINGTON QUAY

CAFE

Offering Breakfast, Lunch, Cakes & Cream Teas. Views of the River Taw. Free Heritage Centre. Open All Year.

W: fremingtonquay.co.uk
T: 01271 268720
E: thefremingtonquaycafe@yahoo.co.uk

Beneath Fremington Parish lie unseen significant clay deposits that have been used for making pottery dating back to the Bronze Age. This high-quality brown clay was prized by local potters, and supported this important industry in Barnstaple, Bideford and Torrington, with decorated wares made from it being distributed all over the West Country, Ireland and the New World.

Leaving the Quay, we cross an iron bridge over Fremington Pill. *A Pill, in this instance, means a small tidal creek or inlet.* Here we enjoy a good view of the disused lime kiln at the water's edge. We can access the kiln, and the foreshore at low tide, from a

footpath where the bridge ends. Leaving Fremington behind, the Trail here is uncharacteristically completely straight for nearly 3km, yet encompasses much of interest. After passing through a cutting, we see more excellent examples of well-managed verges and banks encouraging plant and insect life. Without this work, the banks would soon become a dark thicket of ash, hazel and willow, allowing little light to reach the ground.

Wave Shelter by Geoff Stainthorpe

As the trees lining the Trail thin out, we see a large area of marsh between us and the river; this is Home Farm Marsh, originally wetland that was drained in the 1940s to make the land more viable for agriculture in an effort to help feed the nation.

The land was acquired by the Gaia Trust in 2002, and through low-intensity farming and careful management it is being restored to wet pasture.

The Marsh is well worth a detour off the Trail, but please note that dogs and bicycles are not permitted.

There are three entrances to the site, so if you miss one, there should be another along soon.

There are some fine examples of pollarded

Home Farm Marsh

willows, pollarding being a similar practice to coppicing (regular cutting of fresh tree growth around ground level) but performed several feet up the main trunk, which places new shoots safely out of reach of browsing animals. Newly-grown branches were typically cut between 1-15 years, depending on the tree species and the use to which they were going to be put, from 'tree hay' (animal fodder) to basket-weaving and fence-making, where this practice produced the long, straight poles needed. A beneficial by-product is

Pollarded willows

that trees pruned in this way produce less shading, allowing increased plant and insect diversity at ground level.

Still on this long straight, we begin to make out what appears to be an archway across the Trail. It turns out to be another piece of Trail sculpture in the form of an upturned boat, and is made of locally salvaged materials. As we approach Yelland, there are numerous tidal inlets that come right up to the Trail, and the areas to both sides are valuable feeding and stop-over grounds for migrating birds.

We glimpse an out-of-place grass mound between the Trail and the river; this is the remains of the power station built in 1955 to light up the whole of North Devon and demolished just 30 years later. The huge building was of brick

Roundhouse

construction along the lines of iconic Battersea Power Station on the Thames in London, but had just two chimneys. Coal to fire it was brought by ship from Wales and unloaded at a specially-built jetty out in deep water. The area on which it stood is being steadily reclaimed by Nature, despite the soil containing a range of contaminants.

The gated road we now reach and cross shows another glimpse of the Trail's origins, with some more sections of rail visible in the tarmac.

After we have passed the huge site, the Trail opens out to flat farmland on both sides. Looking in the distance over the river to the north, we see the edge of Braunton Burrows, the largest sand dune system in England and the heart of the Biosphere Reserve. It was notably used for D-Day training during WW2 and in the Pink Floyd film 'The Wall'. Shortly, we see a small roundhouse in the field below the Trail, accessed by steps and located in a delightful picnic area providing benches and tables. The roundhouse walls are built mainly from cob; a mixture of earth, clay, straw and stones that was a very common building material in the area.

Reaching a concrete road, which the Trail crosses, we can make a detour towards the estuary to a small beach where the rivers Taw and Torridge meet before flowing out to sea, and where we have fine views across to solar-powered Crow Point lighthouse, actually a squat metal tower, and Braunton Burrows.

Did you know?
There are two curious slatted white structures, one to the left on the hill as we approach Instow and one to the right on a metal tower. Looking very much like cricket sight-screens, their purpose is to guide shipping up the twisting navigation channel of the river Torridge.

Although quite close by boat, it would require a 21km journey to reach the lighthouse on foot.

If we follow the shoreline or sandy roadway keeping the estuary to our right, we can explore Instow village with its fine beach and facilities, to then rejoin the Trail at Instow level crossing and signal box.

A small military installation to our left, the Royal Marines' Arromanches Camp is used for amphibious trials and training, with hovercraft and landing craft often being seen and heard on the beach and estuary nearby. The Trail here is lined by delightful multicoloured dwellings of various vintages. A stone bridge crossing the trail at an angle carries Marine Parade, Instow's long 'high street'; however, the Trail

Granite waymarker

passes through a deep tree-lined cutting and the village remains largely unseen. We pass under another, smaller bridge before reaching the first and shorter of two tunnels on the Trail where cuttings proved impractical.

Signal at Instow

On bright sunny days, the sudden darkness upon entering the tunnel, especially when cycling, leaves you blinded, so remember to take special care and, as a sign advises, *Remove Sunglasses*. Once through the tunnel, the cutting becomes more shallow, and to our right is a newly-planted micro-orchard from which, when mature, we are invited to pick and eat 'a fair share' of the fruit and nuts the trees will bear. Upon reaching the white level crossing gates and railway signal, we have completed this section of the Tarka Trail.

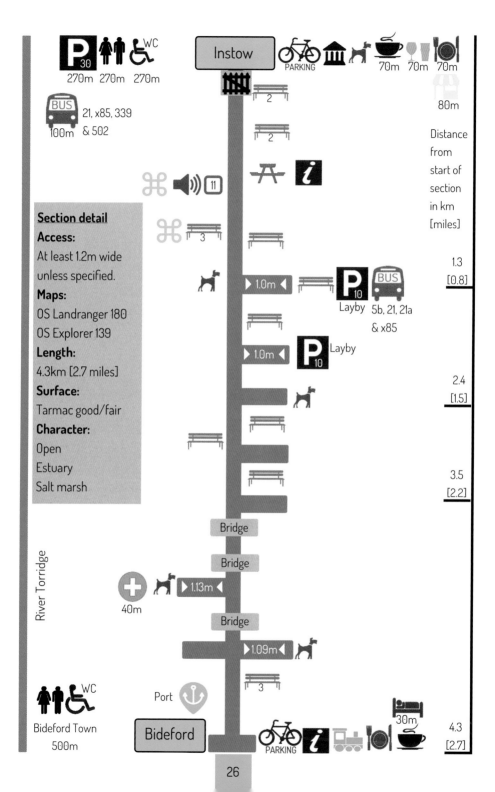

Instow

P₃₀ 270m   👩‍🦽 270m   WC 270m

BUS 100m   21, x85, 339 & 502

PARKING   🏛   🐕   ☕ 70m   🍷 70m   🍽 70m

🏪 80m

Distance from start of section in km [miles]

⌘   ◀))   11

🏕   *i*

Section detail
Access:
At least 1.2m wide
unless specified.
Maps:
OS Landranger 180
OS Explorer 139
Length:
4.3km [2.7 miles]
Surface:
Tarmac good/fair
Character:
Open
Estuary
Salt marsh

⌘   🪑 3

🐕   ▶ 1.0m ◀   🪑   P₁₀   BUS
      Layby   5b, 21, 21a & x85

1.3 [0.8]

🪑

▶ 1.0m ◀   P₁₀ Layby

🐕

2.4 [1.5]

🪑

🪑

3.5 [2.2]

🪑

Bridge

Bridge

➕ 40m   🐕 ▶ 1.13m ◀

River Torridge

Bridge

▶ 1.09m ◀   🐕

🪑 3

👩‍🦽 WC

Port ⚓

Bideford Town 500m

Bideford

PARKING   🚲   *i*   🚂   🍽   ☕   🛏 30m

4.3 [2.7]

Instow to Bideford

Instow is deserving of a detour from the Trail, with its long sandy beach and good local facilities, not to mention the Hockings ice cream van and a seasonal ferry across the river Torridge to Appledore. There are further remnants of track in the road at the old level crossing and beyond, plus another signal

Instow signal box

where the track ends. The award-winning Grade II listed signal box was built in 1874, and its survival is testament to the determination of villagers who saved it from demolition in the early 1980s when the line closed. It is occasionally opened to the public by volunteers in high season, when visitors can see the interior largely as it was when the line closed. The North Devon Yacht Club now occupies one of the old station buildings opposite the remaining platform.

Did you know?
The sand on Instow beach has been over 2m lower than its present level. The sea wall used to be 4m above the beach, and a flight of 13 steps, which are now buried, were needed to reach the sand.

Leaving Instow behind, we pass through a short cutting, lined with overhanging trees creating a natural tunnel, and soon find ourselves at the edge of the river Torridge. The huge sheds housing Appledore Shipbuilders, established in 1855, lie directly across the river, beside the picturesque village of Appledore. Both part-sections and complete vessels are built here, and in 2014 an order for a third 90m-long 1900-ton patrol vessel for the Irish Navy provided a welcome boost to the local economy. Whilst the river becomes narrow and relatively shallow at low water, there can be a tidal range of over 8m at the yard, enabling it to accommodate larger ships. Nearby is a 96m dry dock available to rent, should you wish to repaint your superyacht.

The Trail closely follows the river and eventually passes a jetty, the MOD's Zeta Berth, a small amphibious training facility and home to an incongruous zoo of furry toy animals attached to the security fence. The garden, picnic bench and bird table look equally out of place; however, the thankful birds have no qualms about dining on Defence-owned property. A little further on and beside the road next to us is a fine lodge house seen through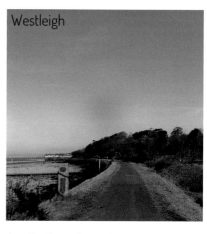

the trees. This marks the entrance to Tapeley Park and Gardens, a 'working farm' stately home open to the public, and owned by larger-than-life protester and campaigner Hector Christie. The elevated position makes it worth visiting for the estuary views alone.

Did you know?
There are over 200 lime kilns around the coast and rivers of North Devon. When limestone is burned in these kilns with wood or coal, lime is produced. Lime is used in building, for mortar and renders, and in agriculture, where it helps neutralise acid soils and improve yields.

We cross several tiny bridges, given away by iron railings, and there are now salt marshes on both sides of the Trail in places. With a high spring tide, the path here lies only a few feet above the water lapping at both sides. Shortly, a shallow protective dyke, breached in places, is seen diverging from the Trail, now creating larger salt marshes fringed with driftwood brought in by only the highest tides. *Explore these areas with extreme caution. The edges are particularly treacherous.*

Approaching Bideford, we can be excused for thinking we have returned to Barnstaple, as the bridge we see is, at first glance, its twin, but in fact is considerably longer and higher. Opened in 1987, it took traffic away from Bideford's 13th century Long Bridge just as the new Taw Bridge in Barnstaple reduced traffic impact on its ancient bridge in 2007. After passing under the bridge, the Trail leaves a shallow cutting behind, and a break in the trees allows superb views of Bideford and the Long Bridge beyond.

Overgrown and almost hidden to the right of a bench is another lime kiln to discover and explore. As buildings begin to line each side of the Trail we have reached Bideford, and this side of the river is known as East-the-Water. We continue under bridges, past back gardens and allotments, and finally see additional platforms on both sides directly before Bideford Station. It is believed that these were built to save first class passengers walking around to the Royal Hotel's main entrance; visitors simply stepped out of their carriages and straight into the hotel. Just across the iron road bridge, raised to allow taller traffic to pass under - hence the hump - we come to Bideford Station itself, which gives us the best impression anywhere on our journey of how the railway must have looked in its heyday.

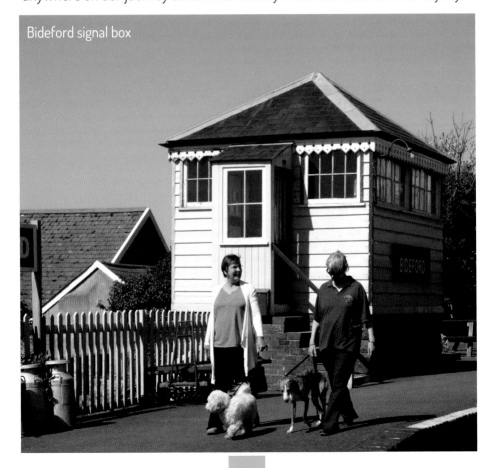

Bideford signal box

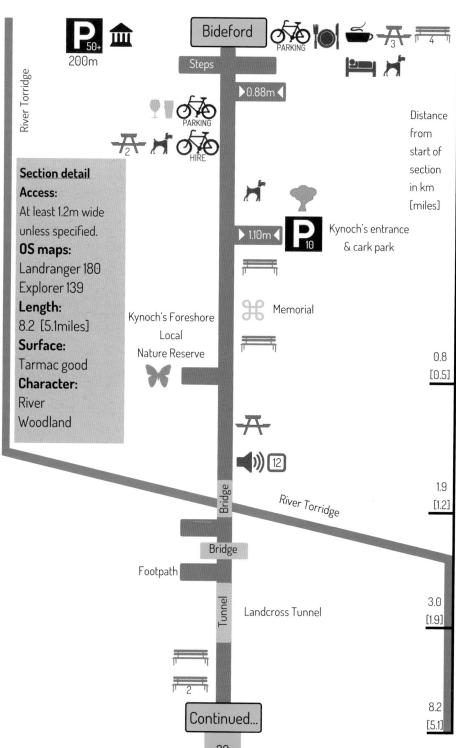

P 50+ 🏛
200m

Bideford

🚲 PARKING 🍴 ☕ 🪑 3 🪑 4

🛏 🐕

Steps

▶0.88m◀

🍷 🚲 PARKING

🪑 2 🐕 🚲 HIRE

🐕

🌳

▶1.10m◀ **P** 10 Kynoch's entrance & cark park

🪑

Section detail
Access:
At least 1.2m wide
unless specified.
OS maps:
Landranger 180
Explorer 139
Length:
8.2 [5.1miles]
Surface:
Tarmac good
Character:
River
Woodland

⌘ Memorial

🪑

Kynoch's Foreshore
Local
Nature Reserve

🦋

🪑

🔊)) 12

0.8
[0.5]

Bridge

River Torridge

1.9
[1.2]

Bridge

Footpath

Tunnel Landcross Tunnel

3.0
[1.9]

🪑
🪑 2

Continued...

8.2
[5.1]

River Torridge

Distance
from
start of
section
in km
[miles]

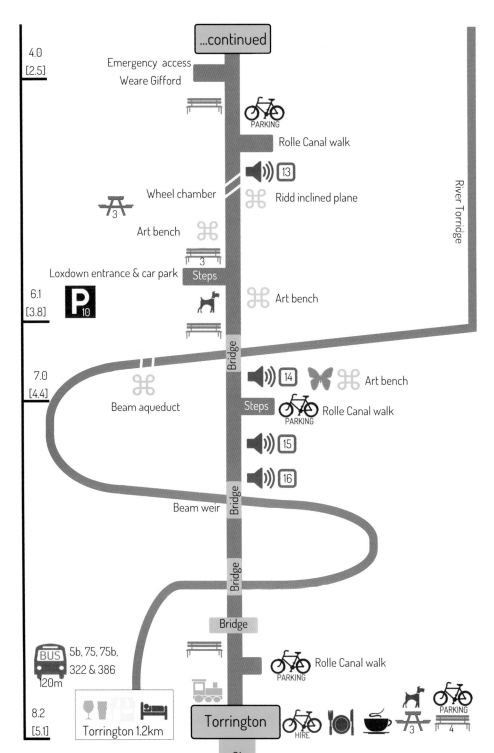

...continued

4.0
[2.5]

Emergency access
Weare Gifford

PARKING

Rolle Canal walk

◀))) 13

Wheel chamber — Ridd inclined plane

3 — Art bench

3

Loxdown entrance & car park — Steps

6.1
[3.8]

P 10 — Art bench

Bridge

7.0
[4.4]

◀))) 14 — Art bench

Beam aqueduct — Steps — Rolle Canal walk
PARKING

◀))) 15

◀))) 16

Beam weir — Bridge

Bridge

Bridge

BUS 5b, 75, 75b,
322 & 386
120m

Rolle Canal walk
PARKING

8.2
[5.1]

Torrington 1.2km — Torrington — HIRE — 3 — 4 PARKING

River Torridge

31

Bideford to Torrington

Bideford is an historic port and was granted a market charter in 1272. The town whose name means '*by the ford*' is mentioned in the Domesday Book, and its first bridge, built from timber in 1286. It was replaced in 1474 by a stone structure that has survived

Bideford Long Bridge

to this day, and is listed as a Grade 1 ancient monument. Despite suffering damage and even partial collapse in its history, it remains a vital river crossing for the town to this day. It is also favoured by roosting starlings, and swirling, swooping clouds of birds in their thousands create a spectacle at dusk, before they dive under the arches to spend the night.

It is surprising to learn that in the 16th century, Bideford was the third largest port in the whole country, and Sir Walter Raleigh landed his first shipment of tobacco here. The wool trade was historically important, and today shipments of clay and timber are exported in special container ships carrying up to 3000 tons. It is quite a spectacle watching one of these 90m-long ships performing a graceful three-point turn on a high tide, before gently sailing out of port under command of a pilot, perhaps bound for Spain, Finland or Holland. The quay as seen today has been lengthened considerably; however, the road and shops along the quay have been under water at least three times that I can remember before flood prevention work. Its height was increased and a new, higher wall built in 2006 to prevent tidal flooding, and this has proved successful to date. The port of Bideford is home to the MS Oldenburg, a 1958 German-built ferry that can carry 267 passengers.

Did you know?
Bideford Long Bridge has 24 stone arches of different widths, and there are several theories why this is, my favourite being that each arch was funded by a different local guild, its width dependant on their wealth.

It provides a lifeline to the residents of Lundy, and the 2-hour sailing also carries tourists to this visually stunning and remote island in the Bristol Channel.

One of Bideford's most famous sons, and cousin of Sir Walter Raleigh, was Sir Richard Grenville, who played a significant role in colonising the New World and fighting against the Spanish. Literary references include *Westward Ho!* by Charles Kingsley, which is set initially in *The Little White Town* as he called it, and, of course, *Tarka the Otter* by Henry Williamson. He lived nearby, and without him we might simply have been exploring *The Old Railway Line*. In the book, Tarka is born in a holt on the river Torridge, 6km upstream, and his journey in the book encompasses many places through which the Tarka Trail now passes. Ironically, when the book was written, otters were still considered vermin.

Bideford Station opened in 1855 as part of an extension southwards from

Tea and cakes on the train

Barnstaple, with regular passenger trains running until 1965. The line remained open for freight until it was finally closed in 1982, with a final rail-tour passenger train passing through in November of that year. The North-West Devon Railway Preservation Society was formed with the intention of preserving the line, but was unable to raise the necessary funding of £313,000, a seemingly paltry sum these days. In 1992, thanks to the hard work of volunteers, 200m of track was re-laid, and the Mk1 Standard Coach, now the cafe, opened in 1994. A Standard Brake Van and a Parcels and Miscellaneous van arrived in 1995, and the latter is now the railway museum and interpretation centre. A Planet 0-4-0 Diesel Locomotive arrived in 2000, and after 4 years of restoration work, in August 2004, it hauled the first passenger train since closure 32 years before.

The station building that remains was originally one of the waiting rooms, with a canopy over the platform. It has been a bank, a cafe, and, most appropriately, home to the Council department which administers the Tarka Trail, however, at the time of writing it is awaiting new tenants. *Please note that the building and the car park are privately owned and the general public are not allowed access.* There is a fine plaque on the wall recording the Tarka Trail's opening in 1992 by H.R.H. The Prince of Wales. Opposite is the delightful signal box complete with levers and indicators; this is a faithful replica of the original, which was demolished in 1970 along with the waiting room that stood beside it. Some of the decorative floor tiles remain, and the area is now used for seating and cycle parking. Once, it was feared the track might be built over, but thankfully the new terrace of cottages was built beside the track in a traditional style.

Leaving Bideford Station behind us, within a few metres we reach more cycle parking and a convenient pub, accessed via steps directly from the Trail. Just past the pub there are extensive elevated views to old

Iron Bridge: photo Tom Hynes North Devon Biosphere

warehousing, and across the river is Bideford's oldest quarter, with many 17th century buildings still standing. We soon leave the hustle and bustle of Bideford behind us, and our journey resumes its peaceful course along salt marshes and the river Torridge. Shortly we come upon a grassy picnic area beside the river, and a little further on the opposite verge lies a modest memorial plaque on a low stone plinth. On 7th March 1945, soon after take-off, an aircraft on a routine flight from nearby Chivenor developed engine trouble and crashed nearby, killing 3 of the 6 crew from the Royal Canadian Air Force.

Kynoch's Local Nature Reserve is a 1.5km-long system of estuarine salt marshes and reed-beds lying alongside the river that was designated in 2011.

Past the memorial, on the opposite side, there is a gap in the trees and an interpretation board; here an elevated boardwalk reaches out into the reserve, and on very high tides the entire area beneath our feet is submerged. A long tree-lined section, mostly oak, leads us to the river crossing known simply as Iron Bridge, where we are rewarded with fine views up and downstream and of the impressive remains of a lime kiln opposite. Crossing the bridge, the Trail climbs almost imperceptibly through a long, shallow, tree-lined cutting until reaching the Trail's second, and longest, tunnel. At 180m long, this horseshoe-shaped stone-lined tunnel follows a curved course, so the exit cannot be seen when entering it. There is adequate lighting, but it can suddenly seem very dark when entering by bicycle on sunny days, so please take care here.

Lime kiln at Landcross

Exiting the tunnel, we notice that the Trail is now at some height above the Torridge, affording excellent views over the flood plain and the Rolle Canal sea lock below us. A canal to take goods further inland than the tidal river allowed was suggested in the 1790s, but it was not until 1823 that the chosen route was surveyed. Work started soon thereafter, and when opened, heavy goods, such as lime and coal, would be transported up the river in barges, through the sea lock, and transferred to smaller flat-bottomed barges known as *tub boats.* These were horse-drawn, typically in strings of six, the leading barge having a pointed bow with the remainder being simple floating boxes, each carrying about 4 tons of cargo. The canal reached inland beyond what is now RHS Rosemoor Gardens, fed by water via a leat from the Torridge at Healand weir.

Did you know?
There was a substantial boatyard near the sea lock, where many boats and ships were built until its closure in 1875, the largest being the Sedwell Jane at 209 tons. It was reported that this ship passed under Bideford Long Bridge, *with only one-and-a-half inches to spare.*

The canal, named after financier Lord John Rolle, was short-lived, and by the 1870s, sections had been sold off, filled in and replaced by the railway. Without the work of the landowners and volunteers from the Rolle Canal Society and Northern Devon Waterways Society, formed in 2003, very little of the lock would have been visible here. Years of heavy clearance, restoration and rebuilding have, literally, brought this area back to life.

The path continues past a gated emergency access point, and shortly after we see to our left bicycle parking and an interpretation board. Here we can enjoy a brief detour to learn more about the canal and its workings. A little further on we come across two curious lines of bricks set into the Trail surface at an angle. These mark the place where tub boats from the Rolle Canal were raised 13m from the floodplain level below to that on which we stand. This change in elevation would conventionally require several locks, but with typical Victorian ingenuity it was achieved quickly in one operation.

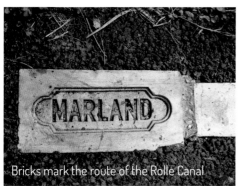
Bricks mark the route of the Rolle Canal

The tub boats were fitted with 4 small iron wheels, and were hauled up rails on an inclined plane with chains powered by an underground water-wheel. Arriving at the higher level, they floated into a canal basin and continued their journey pulled by horses.

As we continue, the village of Weare Giffard with its historic manor house and church are glimpsed through newly-cleared embankments to the left. The road on our right passes over a bridge, and steps from the Trail lead under it to Loxdown, where there is a convenient car parking area.

We soon reach a bridge over the river Torridge, which is becoming noticeably narrower and is now non-tidal fresh water. We have reached, according to the novel, the birthplace of Tarka the Otter, beneath the aqueduct just upstream. This once carried the Rolle Canal over the river Torridge. The 80m-long aqueduct has long been filled in to become a viaduct, and carries the entrance driveway to Beam House, now an adventure holiday centre.

Art Bench by Ben May

Shortly after the bridge is a spectacular bench, and a little further on is bicycle parking with steps leading to a footpath exploring more of the Rolle Canal. This path returns to the Trail quite close to the Puffing Billy, the end of this section, and can be used as an alternative to staying on the Trail. The river follows a more meandering path the further upstream we travel, and we soon cross it again at Beam weir. This was one of our fictional character's favourite places, and is one of only a few locations where I have ever spotted a real otter. The river curves round yet again and we cross a third bridge; here the waters held back by the weir are deeper and slower-flowing. As the height of the embankment that once carried the railway reduces almost to nothing, there is cycle parking and a signed footpath following the Rolle Canal along the hillside and back to the Trail, between the first and second bridges we have just crossed. Climbing a very gentle gradient, we pass under a bridge and reach Torrington Station, now widely known as *The Puffing Billy*, after the pub of that name which opened in the station in the 1990s, and which marks the end of this section.

Interpretation board

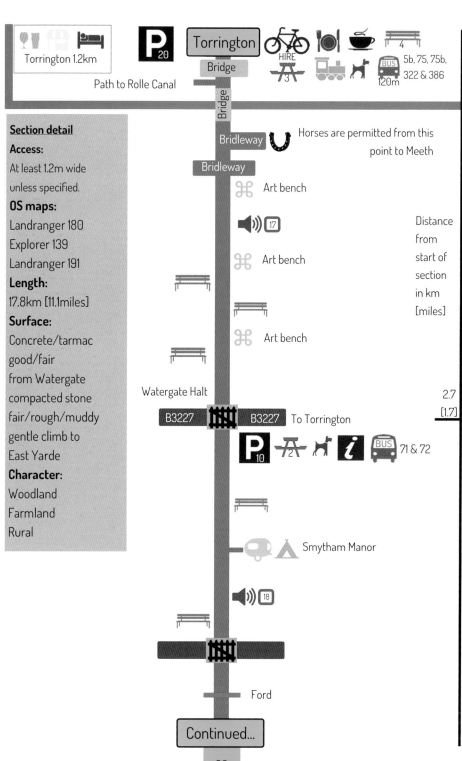

Torrington 1.2km

Path to Rolle Canal

Torrington
Bridge

HIRE

4

5b, 75, 75b, 322 & 386

120m

Bridge

Section detail
Access:
At least 1.2m wide
unless specified.
OS maps:
Landranger 180
Explorer 139
Landranger 191
Length:
17.8km [11.1miles]
Surface:
Concrete/tarmac
good/fair
from Watergate
compacted stone
fair/rough/muddy
gentle climb to
East Yarde
Character:
Woodland
Farmland
Rural

Bridleway

Horses are permitted from this
point to Meeth

Bridleway

Art bench

17

Art bench

Distance
from
start of
section
in km
[miles]

Art bench

Watergate Halt

2.7
[1.7]

B3227   B3227   To Torrington

P 10   72   i   BUS 71 & 72

Smytham Manor

18

Ford

Continued...

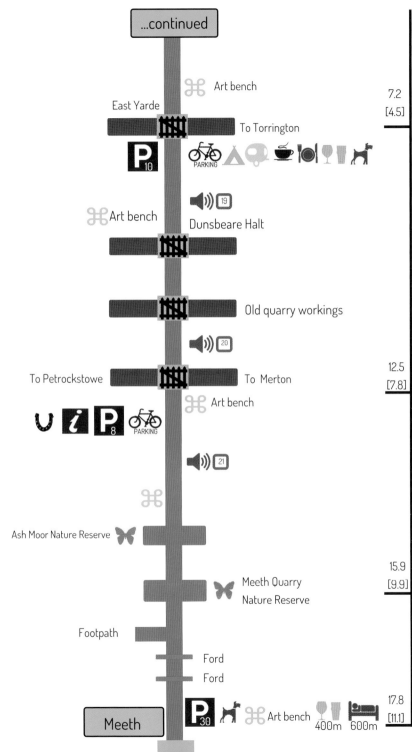

...continued

⌘ Art bench

East Yarde

To Torrington

P₁₀   PARKING

🔊 19

⌘ Art bench

Dunsbeare Halt

Old quarry workings

🔊 20

To Petrockstowe   To Merton

⌘ Art bench

∪ 𝒊 P₈ PARKING

🔊 21

⌘

Ash Moor Nature Reserve

Meeth Quarry
Nature Reserve

Footpath

Ford

Ford

Meeth   P₃₀   ⌘ Art bench   400m   600m

7.2
[4.5]

12.5
[7.8]

15.9
[9.9]

17.8
[11.1]

39

Torrington to Meeth

Torrington Station, in common with many Victorian stations, lies some distance from the town itself. Here, the town is 2km distant and some 70m higher than the station. Opened in 1872, it was originally a passenger terminus, but by 1880 a narrow-gauge freight line connected it to the nearby clay mines and quarries. It was not until 1925 that it was opened up southwards by standard gauge, and it closed to passenger services in 1965. Freight continued to be carried until the early '80s, when the line was closed and the rails lifted. The Tarka Valley Railway group was set up in 2008, and the active membership has been busy re-laying track, clearing overgrown areas and restoring the rolling stock. There are plans to add a short length of track, and a restored carriage now houses a small shop and railway memorabilia. *At the time of writing, Spring 2015, the pub was closed, awaiting new owners; however, it is thought to be opening again shortly.*

The Trail from here to Meeth is far less frequented than the Torrington to Braunton section, and has a considerably more rural and remote feel to it. Leaving the station behind, we pass through the road bridge and very soon on our right is a small archway. Through it and to the left, a path leads down to the Rolle canal, which follows the river Torridge to Taddiport, a settlement on the river below Torrington. Here we are able to walk on the canal bed itself, and there are remains of the retaining wall that once held the water. *There is no short or signposted loop back to the Trail if the canal path is taken.*

40

After a few steps further along the Trail, we reach the start of a long, sweeping iron bridge over the river and surrounding fields, much of which becomes flooded when the river is in spate. Looking downstream, we see the 15th century Grade II listed Rothern Bridge, situated behind the

newer road bridge closest to us. In dry periods, it is difficult to imagine that floodwaters can reach almost to the arch tops of the old bridge. I have stood on this bridge during floods when the water was high enough to wash over the parapets; the reason for building the new, higher road bridge was abundantly clear.

Shortly after crossing the iron railway bridge, an often-muddy farm road crosses our path, and a little further on, a bridleway joins from the left; we now share the Trail with horse riders for the remainder of our journey. Immediately on the left is the first of a series of three sculptures made from old railway sleepers - sadly some had lost their heads when this guide was written. The Trail climbs gently through a narrow, steep-sided valley, following a small river until a platform and gate are reached. This is Watergate Halt, last used in 1982 as a freight line. A local farmer once recounted to me that he, his father and mother would walk to the halt with two full milk churns between the three of them, for delivery to the waiting milk train. In the winter, they would wear socks over their boots to prevent them slipping on the steep road downhill from the farm.

> **Did you know?**
> The local woodcarver who created the series of three benches with figures carved from old railway sleepers on this section is John Butler. He also carved the gigantic wooden hand that holds up a huge low branch on the 'Wonky Conker' tree at the far end of Bideford Quay.

After crossing the road, there is a small car park and picnic benches; here we begin a long climb to the summit of the Trail. Very gentle by walking and cycling standards, the gradient is considerably steeper than most modern railways, and that steam trains were able to operate on it is a marvel. The surface here is compacted gravel and earth; however, the

Did you know?
The maximum speed on the line between Torrington and Meeth was 40kph or less. A 32 km journey using this section of the railway would have taken 80 minutes.

Picnic Bench at Watergate

copious water run-off during wet periods can expose larger stones, so take care. It can safely be cycled on a road bike, as I do; however, a mountain bike will be more comfortable. This section was previously heavily shaded by trees overgrowing the Trail, but it has been opened up considerably by the coppicing and removal of weaker trees, promoting a greater diversity of smaller plants as the sunlight activates dormant seeds. There is the added benefit of keeping the pathway in better condition by allowing it to dry out more quickly. Crossing a narrow country road, we are now two-thirds of the way up the incline, and after crossing a small ford we come across some mosaic sculpture seating constructed by a local school. Trees lining our path become smaller, and as the tree canopy thins, we arrive at Yarde Halt. Originally constructed to serve the nearby clay works, there is now a small car park here opposite a cafe, which can also offer accommodation.

Easter Hall Park Stables
Horse Riding lessons
Tarka Trail hacks
Petrockstow EX20 3HP
01837 810350

A family out for a Sunday afternoon stroll

From the summit of the Trail, at 136m, our route is largely downhill or flat, and leaving East Yarde behind, the surrounding farmland becomes progressively marshy as we descend. The long gradient levels out, and eventually enters a shallow wooded cutting. The single platform located here is Dunsbeare Halt, another stop for the clay works, and opposite the platform is a mosaic sculpture bench in the form of a trio of birds. We cross the small country road beyond, and continue between wooded verges and marshland until another road is reached. Looking left, we can see some of the quarry buildings, now closed, but at its peak, countless thousands of tons of clay left here by train, and later by lorry along this lane.

Here, on one of the least-used parts of the Trail, we can enjoy a feeling of solitude even in peak season. Buzzards are very common in North Devon, and can often be spotted sitting patiently on windless days in lower branches, waiting for prey. The trees often ring to the sound of woodpeckers, which remain largely unseen;

Stowford Cottages
Indoor Pool
400m to Tarka Trail
01805 601487
stowfordlodge.co.uk

however, the noisy jays are less shy, and these colourful birds are easily spotted. Crossing the road we come to Petrockstow Station, throughout its life spelt without the 'e' of the village of Petrockstowe that it once served, nearly a mile distant to the south-west. The line carried passengers from 1925-65, and freight, primarily clay from the nearby quarries, until 1982. This part of the Trail is one of contrasts - light and shade, warmth and coolness - as you pass though dense conifer plantations that open out onto thin coppiced boundaries bordering meadows with longer-reaching views.

Shortly the Trail takes an abrupt ninety-degree turn – not what is expected from a railway line and actually a more recent diversion from the railway's original course to circumnavigate the three hundred and seventy-odd acres of Meeth clay quarries and pits, fairly recently closed to production. Also at this point is a pedestrian-only path to the village of Dolton, some 4 miles to the north-east. From the previously straight or gently curving course, the Trail's character suddenly changes to one of a more meandering nature. It now largely follows the Little Mere River and ancient field boundaries, picking its way through mature stands of conifers and passing by the occasional ancient oak.

Brown hare

Look out for the Ash Moor Nature Reserve interpretation board and access point to the west of the Trail.

A little further on is Meeth Quarry Nature Reserve, the old workings having been purchased by the Devon Wildlife Trust (DWT) and the Reserve established in 2013.   There   is   a delightful picnic area to the west of the trail at this point, with a small pond, interesting benches and totem pole bike parking. Further tracks extend to both sides of the Trail here, with the Nature Reserve lying to the east.

Did you know?
Ash Moor Nature Reserve is culm grassland, which is an area of acidic clay soils supporting boggy grassland and heath. Found only in the south-west of England, Wales, and south-west Scotland, this valuable habitat is noted for its biodiversity.

Alma Farm B & B
5 acre organic smallholding
Approximately 400 m from end of Tarka Trail
Devon Country Garden
01837 811778

It will be most exciting to see how Nature and sympathetic management over the coming years further transform this previously almost sterile environment into a haven for plants and wildlife.

Continuing toward the end of this section, we cross two usually shallow fords that can

Meadow thistle

flood during inclement weather, requiring the use of the raised side paths built above *'high tide'* level. Of course, you could simply splash through. We then reach the steepest hill on our journey, climbing for just a few tens of metres to where the Trail diversion finally rejoins the railway's original course at a wide gate. Here we turn right and can take either the metalled road or, parallel to it, a narrow and undulating unmade path that can be quite muddy in all but very dry spells.

Either route leads us shortly to Meeth Halt, still complete with overgrown platform, station name sign and waiting room, marking the end of the shared-use section of the Tarka Trail and also of our guide.

We hope you enjoyed the Tarka Trail, however much or little you explored, and by which ever mode of transport you chose. It is truly one of North Devon's finest assets, bordering the huge Taw and Torridge estuaries in the north, to the diminutive Little Mere River in the south, the Trail can offer something for everybody: breathtaking landscapes and nature; historic towns; industrial and railway heritage. The Tarka Trail has it all in abundance. And it's free!

Dragonfly

Nearest chemist/ doctor

Braunton
Braunton Health Centre & Lloyds Pharmacy.
150m from Trail.
Caen Street, Braunton,
EX33 1LR. 0844 477 8618.

Bideford
Wooda Surgery & Lloyds Pharmacy 300m
from Bideford Station. Barnstaple St
EX39 4AU. 01237 471071

Fremington
Fremington Medical Centre. 2.7km from
Fremington Quay. Beards Road, Fremington,
EX31 2PG 01271 376655
Chemist 2.7km from Fremington Quay.
6 Higher Rd, Fremington
EX31 3BG. 01271 372407.

Barnstaple
Barnstaple Health Centre. 1.6km from
Barnstaple Station.
Vicarage Street, Barnstaple
EX32 7BH. 01271 371761
Tesco Pharmacy 300m from Barnstaple
Station. Barnstaple Retail Park.
EX31 2AL. 01271 308447

Torrington
Torrington Health Centre. 2.2km from
Torrington Station
New Road, Torrington.
EX38 8EL. 01805 622247.
Lloyds Pharmacy. 2km from Torrington
Station. 1 High Street, Torrington.
EX38 8HN. 01271 862058.

Meeth
Hatherleigh Medical Centre & Chemist.
4.1km from Meeth Halt
Pipers Meadow, Okehampton EX20 3JT.
01837 810283.

Links to local information

North Devon Coast AONB	explorethecoast.org
North Devon Biosphere	northdevonbiosphere.org.uk
Braunton Tourist Information	visitbraunton.co.uk
Barnstaple Tourist Information	staynorthdevon.co.uk
Bideford Tourist Information	bidefordtic@torridge.gov.uk
Torrington Tourist Information	great-torrington.com